Your Money in Your 20s

A Checklist Guide to
Personal Finance

Lisa Duncan

D1113768

Cover designed and illustrated by Sara Dumanske

for my twenty-something daughters

CONTENTS

Your Money in Your 20s

INTRODUCTION

Mind on my money
Money on my mind
Trying to stack paper
Counting every little dime
Down to the penny
Holla if ya hear me
- Flo Rida

I was thirty years old before I put any effort into learning about finances and investing. I didn't have much money at first so I didn't think investing applied to me. When I did have money I was paralyzed by having too many choices. I missed out on investing early in my life.

You have the opportunity to do better than me. You are still in your 20s and I'm going to give you a huge head start on getting your financial affairs in order with good money habits.

Money education isn't a one-time event; it's more like going to the gym. Sometimes you enjoy it, sometimes you dread it, but over time you see results and you are glad you went. Your financial knowledge will build over time, over decades, and that's great because you may be poor now but you will be well prepared for the future when you are rich.

I can't stress enough how important it is to start now. It may feel like your life is already too full with learning a new career, dealing with all the decisions of living independently, maybe even relocating, thinking about insurance for the first time ever, and a host of other challenges. It seems like a lot, so you are wondering if this is the right time to work on financial education.

The answer is yes; this is the perfect time to learn about money. You don't have too much of it so you can't make any huge mistakes. And if you think you are busy now, your thirties are not going to be less complicated. Now is the time to choose the path of financial success and peace of mind.

Is this book for you?

This book is for people starting out in their career who want financial success and a strategy for the future. You might be experiencing these shifts in your life:

Student → Working adult

Part-time → Full-time employee

Living at home or college → Living on your own or planning your exit from home

On your parents' insurance → Choosing your own insurance

Always broke → Earning a salary and wondering where all the money goes

Lots of change means lots of opportunity to set up good systems and habits. I not only want you to be rich someday, I want you to be above average in your financial intelligence.

According to a 2019 survey by Schwab[1], Americans are failing at a lot of basic financial skills:

- 62% have no emergency fund, which means when an emergency expense comes along they have to take a high interest loan or put it on high interest credit cards.

- 44% typically carry a credit card balance, which is a very expensive way to owe money.

---

[1] https://www.aboutschwab.com/modernwealth2019

- Only 28% feel confident about reaching their financial goals.

Meanwhile, half of millennials believe they will be millionaires someday.[2] I hope you do reach that goal, and if that's your plan, then you better know how to manage money. You don't need complicated financial systems in your 20s but you can use this foundational system to prepare yourself for the future.

This book is in the form of checklists because this is stuff that needs to get done without a lot of boring talk, talk, talk. If I haven't given you enough background information to take action then please go look it up on the Internet. I find Wikipedia financial topics very helpful. There are volumes of information out there, which could land you in analysis paralysis, so don't get distracted and don't be fooled by people trying to sell you something.

To keep this book concise, it is focused on single professionals. If you are married, have joined your finances with another, own a house, have children, or any other of those mature adult things that complicate life, you will find this book to be a good starting point but you will also find more information in my book *Your Money in Your 30s*. Master the basics in this book first for a solid financial foundation.

Your relationship with money

Many people I know have a complicated relationship with money. Some fear spending it and some fear missing out by not spend it. Some think it's bad manners to talk about money and some don't know who to talk to. Some people carry a heavy burden of shame attached to their money, whether it's guilt about credit card debt or guilt about having more than other family members. In the words of Buddha: Let that shit go.

---

[2] TD Ameritrade Millennials and Money survey, 2018

Money is just a tool, like your smart phone and your Instant Pot, which exists to serve your needs without distracting from the important things in your life. Money is not a scoreboard for the quality of your life and it's not the magic path to happiness. We want to manage it in a way that we maximize it as a resource and minimize the effort to do that.

The most important thing is to just get started. Doing something is far more likely to earn you money than doing nothing. We are not striving for perfection here. We are going to make sensible choices and let them ride for a while. Everything we do can be changed as your priorities and knowledge change. So approach this with no fear, no shame, and no negative baggage.

As you complete these checklists you will get more comfortable talking about money. I encourage you to work through this book with a friend so you can support each other and celebrate your progress. I want to assure you that whatever level of trepidation you are feeling will dissipate as you continue to take steps forward. I am cheering for you.

Assess your current knowledge and needs

Use this checklist to assess your current money management skills. This book will help you achieve all the things on this list. If you are succeeding on everything here then you have a good financial start and you may want to move on to the next book: *Your Money in Your 30s*.

Spending
- ☐ I have a job
- ☐ I spend less than I make
- ☐ I know my budget (fixed expenses, saving, flexible spending)
- ☐ I know how long it will take to pay off my debts (student, car, credit card)

Saving

- ☐ I have an emergency fund that could provide 3-6 months of living expenses if I were unemployed.
- ☐ I have a savings plan for my next major purchase
- ☐ I contribute to a retirement fund
- ☐ I take full advantage of any 401(k) match my company offers
- ☐ I know if I qualify for a Roth IRA and I contribute to it
- ☐ My money is automatically moved from my paycheck to the appropriate savings accounts

Banking

- ☐ My paycheck is auto-deposited to my bank account
- ☐ I have a debit/checking account with no monthly fee
- ☐ All my bills are paid automatically and on time
- ☐ I pay my credit card bills in full every month
- ☐ I know what interest rate I am earning on my accounts

Investing

- ☐ I have an investment account at a brokerage
- ☐ I have an investment strategy
- ☐ My investments do not make me anxious
- ☐ I review my investments on a regular basis

Credit Rating

- ☐ I annually check my credit report for errors
- ☐ I know my current credit score
- ☐ I know what to do to improve my credit score

Taxes

- ☐ I am current with my income tax filings and payments

This is the day

Now is the best possible moment in your life to work on your finances. Good decisions today will compound for decades. Doing nothing means inflation eats away at the spending power of your savings, so you are actually falling behind. You can do better than that.

DOING NOTHING = LOSING MONEY

Let's get excited about moving forward. Imagine how great it would feel to be able to say

- I am confident I can pay for what I need on a daily basis and in the case of a cash emergency.
- My debt is under control and I am building a good credit rating.
- I am saving for both my retirement and more near term goals.
- My investment choices are aligned to my financial goals and do not cause me stress.
- I am in control of my money and confident in my choices.

Try this:
- ☐ Brainstorm your own financial goals. Think both short term and long term. What would you like to do during your life? When would you like to retire? How much money would meet your needs?

Now that you have some big goals in mind, we'll get you on the path to reach them.

Take the next step

The good news is that financial management isn't very hard. There are lots of people out there who would like to sell you complicated products and charge you lots of money, but you don't need them. Common sense and a simple plan will earn you great rewards. By the time you finish this book you will have the answers to these questions:

1. Where is all my money going?
2. What kind of savings do I need and where do I keep it?
3. Can I pick the right investments?
4. What is my credit score and does it matter?
5. What part of this is fun???

Making decisions isn't always fun, but sitting back and seeing your bank accounts grow can be quite enjoyable. We are going to make that happen with a minimal amount of effort.

1

SPENDING

You have money coming in and going out of your bank account all the time and if you are like most people you aren't exactly sure how it gets used up so fast. We are going to dig a little to make a summary view of where your money is going and check whether that matches your goals. We will set up your payment and saving systems so it is easy to spend and save without having to stress over the details every day. You will know how much you have to spend for fun while saving happens in the background.

Do I need a budget?

Our budget goal is to minimize waste and maximize fun. If your budget reveals that you spend $500 per month on avocado toast, I'm not going to tell you to stop, I'm going to ask: Is that more important than other ways you could spend $500? If it brings you great joy then we will build it into the budget. On the other hand, if your budget reveals you are paying a lot for something you don't care strongly about, I will challenge you to cut that expense.

This is all about making your money achieve what you want. With a good understanding of where your money goes, you can make good decisions to balance your short-term and long-term goals.

My take-home pay

Take a look at your paycheck stub. Are you paid weekly, bi-weekly, monthly, or by commission or tips? Whatever it is, figure out your typical monthly take-home pay after taxes and benefit co-pays have been deducted.

When you started your job your employer had you fill out a Form W-4 to establish how much in taxes they would withhold from your check. If you have one job and no unusual deductions then the form probably estimated your taxes correctly. If you have multiple jobs, other sources of income, or lots of tax adjustments, you may need to adjust your paycheck withholding.

Check your tax withholding:

☐ If you filed a tax return last year and your refund or payment was small, and you've had no big changes in income this year, your withholding is probably good enough and you can skip the next step.

☐ If your situation is more complicated and you want to check that your paycheck tax withholding is correct for your income, use the **IRS Withholding Calculator** (online at irs.gov). Adjust your withholding if you need to by getting a W-4 form from your payroll department.

How much do I spend?

As a young, tech-savvy adult, you can use technology to make the process of tracking your spending easier. The first thing you need is the raw data of where you are currently spending your money. Choose a tracking and categorization method that works for you.

- Use an app like Mint by Intuit to feed in your debit, credit card and bank account transactions for a summary by category of all your spending. It will let you change the categories if it guesses wrong and you can add cash transactions manually if you want.
- If you don't want to link your accounts to an app or you mostly use cash, try a phone app designed for easily tracking your spending and use if for one month.
- Or, if you like spreadsheets, look through all your accounts and transactions from the last month and categorize them yourself.

Understand where your money goes:
   ☐ Categorize one month of typical spending using any tool of your choosing.

The end result will be your monthly budget starting point. It won't be perfect because change is constant, but it will be good enough for now. Let's see where you are and start making adjustments to make your life better. Some expenses aren't monthly, such as car repairs and special events, so we'll make a miscellaneous category to estimate those.

Budget Worksheet

Now that you have your numbers collected, let's see how it all fits together. Complete the following table with all the information you currently have.

I'm going to ask you to enter some estimated savings goals. If you currently live a lifestyle where you spend everything you make, this plan will create upheaval in your life. If you make barely enough to survive, then proactive action is needed to change your income or expenses. If you spend everything you make because you are buying crap and going out, it's time to make some choices. Do you want to be broke forever or do you want to build a financial future?

Let's be optimistic and start with some kind of allocation for all the savings goals. If that leaves you with a negative monthly balance, we'll have to dial it back. But I hope that after you read the "Saving" chapter you will be so excited about saving that you will revisit this budget worksheet and allocate even more to savings.

My Budget Worksheet

Income	Monthly $
Take-home pay (after taxes & co-pays)	
Other income	
Total monthly income	

Fixed Expenses	Monthly $
Rent	
Utilities (water, gas, electricity, garbage)	
Cell phone	
Internet, cable, Netflix, Hulu, etc.	
Other subscriptions & memberships	
Groceries	
Car payment	
Gas, parking, public transportation	
Insurance (auto, renters, disability)	
Health insurance (not covered by workplace)	
Student loan payment	
Credit card debt payment	
Charitable giving	
Other	
15% of income for miscellaneous [3]	
Total monthly fixed expenses	

---

[3] "miscellaneous" is an estimate for all the things that are hard to capture on a per month basis but are necessary, like haircuts, dry cleaning, car maintenance, gifts, pet expenses, etc.

Savings Allocation	Monthly $
Emergency fund (start with 5% of income)	
401(k) to maximize employer match	
Roth IRA (at least 5%, up to $500/month) [4]	
Future goal fund (try 5% of income) [5]	
Total monthly savings allocation	

Put it all together (from above)	
Total monthly income	
Minus total monthly fixed expenses	-
Minus total monthly savings allocation	-
Available monthly flexible spending	

Fantastic, you now have a budget estimate that allows you to examine where your money is going and make adjustments to your spending and saving. While the fixed expenses seem unavoidable and saving feels like a chore, flexible spending is where things start to get interesting and enjoyable.

Monthly flexible spending includes all the things you have control over and can choose how much and how often you do them. This spending is connected to your desires and your vision of your future. It includes possibilities like:

---

[4] If you qualify for a Roth IRA, which we will determine in the "Saving" chapter.
[5] We'll talk about the Future goal fund in the "Saving" chapter.

- Fun things
  - Eating out and food delivery
  - Entertainment - movies, concerts, gaming, events
  - Vacation - transportation, lodging, sightseeing, activities
  - Clothes, shoes, accessories
  - Manicures, pampering, luxury experiences
  - Home goods, hobbies, gifts, optional subscriptions
- Pro-active debt reduction
  - If you have high interest debt, we're going to talk about the value of getting that paid off.
  - If you have low interest loans, you can decide if you are the type of person that gets joy from paying off their loans faster.
- Investing
  - This is the part where you make yourself rich by making your money work for you.

Calculate your % flexible spending

Available monthly flexible spending divided by *Total monthly income* will give you your flexible spending percentage.

_____ / _____ x 100 = _____% flexible spending

If your available flexible spending is between 10% and 30%

☐ Pat yourself on the back; you are earning well and have your fixed expenses under control.

☐ Do you want to put a little more into savings? Embracing the saving habit is the key to becoming rich.

If your available flexible spending is between 0% and 10%

☐ You don't have much spare income so you must live frugally to avoid debt. Find free and cheap activities. The market for used clothes, furniture, and other goods has never been easier to navigate. Be creative with how you shop.

☐ Can you make more money by asking for a raise, changing jobs, or working more? You are young and now is the time to hustle.

☐ Can you cut any expenses? Review your budget with a critical eye.

☐ You have little flexibility if a big expense should arise so building up your emergency fund is especially important.

If your available flexible spending is negative, it means you don't make enough money to pay your expenses and save at the rates we proposed. This is challenging but not impossible. Let's strategize. Your number one goal is to avoid taking on credit card debt. It is so expensive that it will continuously drain your resources and keep you from balancing your budget. Try every other strategy before using your credit card.

☐ Make a plan to increase your income by making more money in your current job, by changing jobs, or by working multiple jobs.

☐ Try some of the **Ideas to cut expenses** (below) and be aggressive.

☐ Change the "Future Goal" fund to zero. That goal will have to wait a little longer.

☐ Decrease the Roth IRA allocation. This really hurts me because Roth IRAs are so awesome, as I will explain in the Savings chapter.

☐ I hope you don't need to cut the Emergency fund allocation because this is your safety net and you just don't know what life will throw at you. But do not take on credit card debt in order to put money in your Emergency fund.

☐ Keep making adjustments until you can get your Available flexible spending to be positive.

If your flexible spending is greater than 30%, good for you. You have lots of choices.

☐ You have a lot of disposable income so it's time to do some deep thinking about what you want your money to do for you. You are an ideal candidate to start an investment account and let your money make money. More on that in the "Investing" chapter.

Ideas to cut expenses

Review your spending from time to time and see if your priorities have changed or better priced services have become available. Reducing the cost of a monthly expense will really add up over the years.

☐ Rent is most people's biggest single expense and the hardest one to change in the short term. But if you think yours is out of proportion with the rest of your budget, start thinking about downsizing or having more roommates.

☐ Your car, and all the associated expenses of gas, parking, repairs and insurance, could be up to 30% of your budget. If you are lucky enough to live in a city with good public transportation, consider living without a car. Services like Zipcar are making this choice highly feasible.

☐ Find a new cell phone carrier. In the old days, there were very few cell phone service providers and most of us signed up with one of the big companies who charge too much and lock us into multi-year plans. Now there are many more choices and price points.

  o If you are locked into a plan, look up the expiration date and put it on your calendar so you can revisit this topic.

  o Ask your friends if they are using an alternate carrier that they like.

  o Do some Internet research on carriers in your area.

  o Look up your old bills and figure out how much data your really use per month so you are prepared to choose the cheapest plan that meets your needs.

  o Before you break up with your carrier, grab pdf copies of your last few bills in case they cut off your account access. Your service is probably paid monthly in advance, so when you break up they will owe you the prorated amount of the unused month. (I had to contact my provider four times to get my refund.)

☐ Internet and media services (cable, Netflix, etc.) are essential to most people and can get quite expensive as you opt into more choices. If you are subscribing to something that you rarely use, let it go.

☐ If you think you are paying too much for auto insurance, shop around. Frugal people compare prices once a year.

  o Ask your auto insurance carrier if there are any discounts you are eligible for. There might be a discount if your car and renters insurance are through the same carrier.

  o Increasing your insurance deductible will lower your premium, but make sure you have enough in your emergency savings to cover the deductible amount.

☐ Read your bank statement. The whole thing every month. If you are paying ATM fees, bouncing checks, paying for overdraft or paying a maintenance fee, stop it! Find a better bank. (More on that in the Banking chapter.)

☐ Do NOT cancel your health insurance to save money. If you are uninsured, one serious health event could wipe out everything you've saved and put you into debt for years to come. You would be risking both your health and fiscal ruination. Be a savvy consumer and shop around for the cost and benefits that work for you.

☐ Do NOT cancel your disability insurance to save money. This may be provided by your workplace, but if you are an independent contractor you need to purchase your own disability insurance. You are young and may feel invincible, but unexpected things happen to people of all ages. Think about how you would get by if you could not work for a few months or a few years. Protecting your income is a high priority.

Paying off debt

Debt isn't necessarily a bad thing. There are different types of debt that achieve different goals.

- Student debt = a path to your education that will hopefully lead to better jobs in a field of your choice for better pay. Current federal rates range from 5% to 7.6%

- Car debt = a path to car ownership with a limited time frame, usually 3-5 years. Interest rates are currently around 4% and up.

- Mortgage debt = entry into home ownership, impossible without debt, and leading to a good thing, i.e., the outright ownership of your home, eventually. Fixed interest rates have been low, between 3% and 6% for the past 10 years.

- When monthly payments are made on time and in full, these kinds of debt help your credit rating because they add to your variety of credit.

But then there is credit card debt.
- Credit card interest rates are sky high
- Credit card debt can go on forever
- Carrying credit card debt hurts your credit rating
- Credit card debt = steaming pile of poop

Credit card debt

If you don't like to throw away your money, credit card debt must be eliminated as soon as possible. It is a drain on your finances and your mental energy. Some people feel so guilty about their credit card debt that they can't bear to look at their monthly statements. Instead of feeling guilty, get mad and stop letting those credit card companies make a profit off you. We are going to systematically beat down that debt and get rid of it forever.

- ☐ If you have credit card debt, go back to your budget and increase the amount you are allocating toward paying it off. Move all your savings allocations into the credit card payment category. Saving and investing can't earn you as much as you are losing by paying credit card fees and interest. Move most your flexible spending into the credit card payment category. Be aggressive. The cost of that debt is weighing you down and keeping you from being free.
- ☐ If you are carrying multiple credit card balances, direct the most money to the one with the highest interest rate.
- ☐ If you have multiple debts, of any type, continue to pay your minimum monthly payments on all of them. Missing payments is very bad for your credit rating.

☐ Stop using your credit cards until the debt is paid off. Cut up the cards or put them in a hard to access place, like inside a block of ice. Don't cancel them but don't touch them, they are poison.

Student debt

If you have student loan debt, take advantage of the flexibility offered.

☐ Most student loan servicers will reduce your rate by 0.25% if you sign up for automatic payments.

☐ Research the types of repayment plans designed to fit different income situations at www.studentaid.gov.

☐ If you have multiple loans, investigate rolling them into one loan with a lower interest rate. Note that you might lose the repayment plan flexibility offered by the federal program, so carefully consider your ability to pay the new loan.

Understand your debt outlook

Face your debts with your eyes wide open. The more you know, the better choices you can make. Use a Debt Repayment Calculator, such as the one at www.creditkarma.com/calculators/debtrepayment, to understand exactly when you will pay off each of your debts.

☐ For each debt you have, complete this form:

Debt Name: _____

Enter into online debt calculator:
Balance Owed _____
Interest Rate _____
Monthly Payment _____

Calculator will tell you:
Expected Payoff Time _____

☐ Put your debt payoff dates on your calendar and celebrate when the day arrives!

☐ Each time you hit a debt payoff milestones, look at your budget and adjust. Without that debt payment hanging over you, you will have more money to work with, which is a wonderful problem to have. Apply those extra dollars to your next debt repayment or your savings. You are making great progress!

Spending summary

Hooray, you are done with your budget. You have figured out your fixed spending, reflected on debt reduction, and made a plan to save some money, too. This is a great starting point for your financial journey. When you read the "Saving" chapter you may want to come back and adjust your savings allocations.

You have completed this spending checklist:

- ☐ I know the amount of my after-tax take home pay.
- ☐ I have a good estimate of my monthly fixed expenses.
- ☐ I have a draft allocation for my different types of savings (which we will review and adjust in the next chapter).
- ☐ I have reviewed ways to cut expenses and have maximized my flexible spending.
- ☐ I know how long it will take to pay off my debts.
- ☐ If I have credit card debt, I have an aggressive plan to pay it off.

2

SAVING

Why bother, you might be asking yourself. When you start at zero it's hard to see how saving money is going to help you. Saving for later means giving up something right now and that can be hard to do. If we were good at making moment-by-moment decisions on things that are good for us there wouldn't be a million diet and exercise books. It's hard making good decision over and over. That's why automated saving is the key. We are going to set up our saving system and let it do all the work.

Does this describe you?
- ☐ I want to be able to afford the things that are important to me.
- ☐ I want to feel confident I have the funds to handle an emergency.
- ☐ I want to have enough money that I never feel trapped in my life. I have the freedom to move cities or change jobs.
- ☐ I want to have enough money to make healthy decisions, from the food I eat to medical help if I need it.
- ☐ I want to retire some day when I'm not too very old.

I want all these things for you, too. They all require that you take some of your hard earned money and set it aside. In the beginning it may be small amounts, and that's okay because we are practicing the saving habit. As your income increases, the amount you save should increase. The magic formula is to start early in your life, saving a little all the time, and let your earnings compound and grow into large amounts.

Here is a numerical example to illustrate the compounding benefit of starting your saving habit early in your life. Lets say you want to have $1 million in your bank account when you turn 65 and you have a long term investment that averages 8% growth per year. Which saving strategy looks easiest to you?

Starting at the age of	Save this much per month
20	$189
30	$433
40	$1044
50	$2862

This illustrates how putting off saving makes it harder and harder to catch up with your long-term savings goals. That $189 looks like a lot to save when you are 20 years old but it sure will be easy to do in your 40s and 50s. The important thing is to start now, regardless of how big or small that amount might seem.

The language of savings accounts

There are lots of reasons to save money and lots of ways to do it. Let's review the vocabulary so we can talk about this.

Retirement savings plans get a special deal from the IRS. They grow tax-free until you withdraw from the account, as long as you wait until age 59½ to start making withdrawals. The 401(k), 403(b) and Traditional IRA all allow you to contribute pre-tax dollars, so both the principal and earnings will be taxed when you withdraw them during your retirement. All three have serious penalties for withdrawing money early.

Pre-tax dollars are money you put into an account and that amount is deducted from your taxable income. For example, if you make $60,000 this year and you put $5,000 in a 401k, your employer will report your taxable income for the year was $55,000. This reduces your federal, state and local taxes, so it can really add up. That's not to say you never pay taxes on that money. Taxes are due when you withdraw the money, presumably during your retirement.

After-tax dollars are the opposite of pre-tax dollars, that is, you've already paid income tax on that money. You won't have to pay tax on it again later when you withdraw it.

Types of Savings Accounts

Savings Type	Definition	Where you bank it
Emergency fund	Money you would need for daily living if you lost your job or to deal with a sudden crisis, like fixing your car.	Regular savings account or a money market fund for easy access
Future goal fund	Any expensive item you plan to pay for in the future (e.g. car, house, wedding, vacation)	A bank or brokerage
Roth IRA	Retirement savings of after-tax dollars. Earnings will never be taxed. Income limits apply.	Your own financial institution or your employer might sponsor a plan

Savings Type	Definition	Where you bank it
Traditional IRA	Retirement plan that allows pre-tax contributions. Only for people who don't have access to a 401k.	A bank or brokerage
401(k)	Employer sponsored retirement savings plan that allows pre-tax contributions.	Employer will choose who administers it
403(b)	Tax-sheltered annuity for public school and non-profit organization workers.	Employer will choose who administers it
Investment accounts	This is the rest of your money, the after-tax cash that you are accumulating to invest and grow.	Brokerage account

What type of savings do I need?

There are lots of account choices, many more than listed in the previous table, but as a person in their 20s, these choices should cover what you need at this point in your life.

Emergency Fund

A majority of Americans shockingly have less than $1000 in their emergency fund, leaving them unprepared for a cash emergency. A surprise car repair or temporary unemployment could happen to any of us and will be far easier to manage if you don't have to borrow money or max out your credit cards. Popular opinion is to stash away 3 to 6 months of living expenses.

☐ Write down your Emergency Fund goal:

Monthly fixed expenses $_____ x ____ months = $_____

That may seem like a lot of money right now but you are going to build up that fund over time so it won't be painful at all. In the Budget chapter we allocated 5% of your income to the Emergency Fund. It will take years to fully fund this account, which is okay if your job and living situation are stable. If your situation is not stable and this makes you nervous, you can allocate a larger percentage and reach your goal faster.

401(k)/403(b)

You only have access to a 401(k) or 403(b) retirement savings account through an employer. They decide who administers the account, what the fees are, and what investment choices you are offered. Your money goes in pre-tax, which means it lowers your taxable income and saves you on federal, state and local income taxes. Taxes are delayed until you withdraw the money during your retirement.

> 401(K) MATCH IS AWESOME.
> TAKE THE FREE MONEY!

If your employer matches 401(k) contributions you are being offered a fantastic deal. Let's say they will match up to 3% of your income with a 25% match and you earn $40,000. That means if you contribute $1200 they will throw in an extra $300. You just instantly made a profit of 25% on your pre-tax investment, which is near impossible to do with any other investment. That's too good an offer to pass up. That's why your 401(k) match is a top priority for your overall savings strategy.

401(k) checklist

☐ Find out if your company has a 401(k) program with matching.

☐ If yes, set up your contributions to maximize the match offer.

☐ Don't contribute any more than that amount for now, we have even better places to put your money.

Note that I'm not encouraging you to put more into your 401(k) at this time because of your particular situation as a young twenty-something early in your career. These are my reasons:

1. The 401(k) lets you postpone taxes, but you are at a lower tax rate now than you will be later in your life when you are earning a higher salary. It's probably better to be taxed now and not later.

2. If your salary grows, you will eventually be disqualified from making a Roth IRA contribution, so now is the time to direct your dollars to the Roth rather than a 401(k).

3. You may be saving for a house down payment and those dollars are better directed to a saving/investment account than a 401(k). Some companies allow you to "borrow" money from your own 401(k) and pay it back to yourself on a schedule. If you lose or leave your job you will have to pay it back much faster, on the order of 60 to 90 days. So it is possible to get money from your 401(k) for a house down payment but it is much less flexible than from a non-retirement account or a Roth IRA.

4. If you have extra money after paying down debt and putting away sufficient savings, then sure, go ahead and put more into your 401(k). That would be awesome.

Finally, never cash out your 401(k) before age 59½. You will pay taxes plus penalties thus greatly depleting its value. If you change jobs, do a direct rollover from you old company 401(k) to the new company 401(k) or to a Traditional IRA account you set up at a brokerage.

Roth IRA

I'm going to push hard for you to open a Roth IRA because it is a special kind of savings account that makes a ton of sense right now in your life. In general, every dollar you have is either taxed when you earn it or taxed when you withdraw it from your account. You can't avoid the taxman, except in this particular case. After-tax dollars go into the Roth IRA but everything it earns is yours tax-free.

Let's say you open a Roth IRA right now and contribute $500 per month for 5 years for a total of $30,000. Then you stop, but you leave it in there, invested in something that earns an average of 5% per year. Your initial investment was $30,000. Thirty years after your first contribution, that account will be worth $112,000. At age 59 ½ you can withdraw as much as you want and the $82,000 in earnings will never be taxed. No other type of retirement savings has that amazing feature.

Another benefit of the Roth IRA is that the principal (your contributions) are always accessible to you. If circumstances should change and you need that money, you can withdraw the principal tax-free and penalty-free. You just can't touch the earnings until you are 59 ½ or meet one of the other qualifications. This is unlike every other type of retirement account where your contributions cannot be touched.

To get going on your Roth IRA:
- ☐ Check your eligibility for contributing to a Roth IRA by looking up the income limits for this year. For example, in 2019 a single filer with annual income up to $122,000 can contribute up to $6000. If your income is between $122,000 and $137,000 you can contribute less than $6000

according to a formula. If you make over $137,000 you can't do a regular Roth IRA but you might be able to do a "Back Door Roth IRA", which is a whole other topic you might want to investigate. Before contributing to a Roth IRA look up the current income limits to see if you qualify. (en.wikipedia.org/wiki/Roth_IRA)

☐ Find out if your employer sponsors a Roth IRA account. Check the fees and investment choices. If you like what they offer, this is a really convenient way to have automatic payroll deduction deposited right into the account.

☐ Try really, really hard to hit your maximum annual contribution limit for your Roth IRA.

Traditional IRA

Your annual IRA limit applies to the combined total of your Traditional and Roth IRA contributions. Therefore, a Traditional IRA only makes sense for you if your company has no 401(k) plan and you make too much money to qualify for a Roth IRA. In that situation you can contribute to a Traditional IRA and get the tax benefit.

A Note to the Self-Employed

If you are working as a contractor or run your own business, don't miss out on the opportunity to take a tax deduction and fund your retirement. You won't have a company to manage your 401(k) but you do have options. There are various self-employment retirement plans, including SIMPLE IRA, SEP-IRA and Solo 401(k), all described and compared in IRS Publication 560. This would be a good time to work with an accountant or financial advisor familiar with the choices and required forms.

Future Goal Fund

This is the fun part, thinking about what amazing things you would like to be able to pay for in the future. It could be something happening in the next year, like a vacation, or a few years out, like a wedding or house down payment. Perhaps you need to save for a car down payment or would like to pay for the car outright without taking a loan. How would you save that much?

☐ Write down some of your savings goals.
☐ Do some research to ensure you are realistic about the total cost.
   ☐ If you are saving for a new car, ask your insurance carrier how much your premiums will increase.
   ☐ If you are planning for a wedding, double your guess. Just kidding. Sort of.
   ☐ If you are saving for a house, the down payment should be at least 10%.

☐ Use a "Savings Goal Calculator" on the Internet and find out how much you would need to save per month. (Try www.dinkytown.net for a savings goal calculator.)

Future Goal #1 _____

Amount of money I will need $_____

# of months until I need it _____

According to the goal calculator, I need to save

$_____ per month

☐ Adjust your Future Goal savings allocation in your budget

Investment Account

If you have planned for all the savings above and still have more money to save, then hooray for you. You are ready to start investing and letting your money make money for you, just like the wealthy people do. It's not an exclusive club. It just takes a little effort to set up your investment account and make some investment decisions, which we will talk about in the next two chapters.

Saving summary

Congratulations, you've gone from zero savings to being a savings guru. The more you save, the more control you will have over your life and the more powerful you will feel. Remember, every billionaire started by saving his or her first dollar, so you are right on track.

Let's review your new knowledge and accomplishments:
- ☐ I have a plan to build an Emergency Fund.
- ☐ I am taking advantage of all 401(k) matching offered by my workplace.
- ☐ I have determined if I am qualified for a Roth IRA and allocated money towards it.
- ☐ I have a future goal of something big I would like to purchase and I know how much it costs and how long it will take to save that much.
- ☐ I have adjusted my budget to reflect these savings goals.

3

BANKING

Now that you know what you want to do with your money, it's time to bank like a grown-up, but not necessarily like your parents. I'm not a fan of the well known "brick and mortar" banks (those banks you see on every corner which have been around for a long time, but are known to charge high fees and screw over their customers. Do an Internet search on "banking scandals" for a glimpse of how prevalent this is.) There are much better choices than those big banks.

Banking choices have expanded dramatically since your parents opened their first accounts. Credit unions, brokerages, and online banks offer alternatives with lower fees, higher interest, and a less scummy reputation. Big banks sometimes offer cash incentives to open new accounts or high introductory interest rates, but weigh those benefits carefully against hidden fees and penalties.

You will need multiple accounts, probably at multiple institutions. You may already have some of these set up:

- Checking account for paycheck deposit, paying bills, and your debit card
- Savings accounts for your emergency and future goal fund

- 401(k) or 403(b) account administered by your workplace
- Roth IRA account, possibly administered by your workplace
- ESPP brokerage account selected by your workplace (if you participate in the employee stock purchase plan or receive stock or options as part of your compensation)
- Investment account at a brokerage

That's a lot of accounts to set up and keep track of. We'll talk about each one and choose what fits your lifestyle right now. Some of these may change as you get older and that's fine.

Banking basics

The first things you need are a checking account and savings account, most likely at the same institution so it's easy to transfer money between the two. Your choice should meet these criteria:

☐ No monthly or annual service fee

☐ No minimum account balance

☐ ATMs that are convenient for you

If you like your current bank and are not paying fees, you can stay with them. But if you are paying account service fees, seriously consider switching banks. Breaking up with your bank is hard work, but paying those fees is just insulting. I will give you some good alternatives to the usual banks.

As you accumulate money you will need more options than what most banks and credit unions can offer you. Your different account types will have different goals that require different investment strategies in order to maximize your returns.

I have used all the banking options in the table below and they each served me well for what I needed at the time. If you have never had a bank account, then a Credit Union or Online Bank are going to be the easiest way to get started. They are well suited for a simple financial situation -- checking and savings -- with no threat of hidden fees and penalties (but do read the fine print before signing up). I'm currently a huge fan of the Charles Schwab Checking Account with no fees, no minimum balance, and you can use any bank ATM *for free*. The downside is that the application form is long and the checking account must be linked to a brokerage account with a $1000 minimum or $100/month automatic investment. If you can brave the paperwork, this is a great option that will meet your needs for a long time with their vast array of account types and investment choices.

Types of Financial Institutions

Financial Institution	Pros	Cons
Online Banks have no branch offices, which saves them on costs, which translates to benefits for you.	No fees. Better interest on savings accounts than most others. Very easy to open an account online.	No branch offices, so you need to be comfortable with doing everything online. Check if their ATMs are convenient for you.
Credit Unions are not-for-profit financial groups that offer checking, savings, ATMs, IRAs, CDs, loans.	No fees. Good rates on car loans. Better interest on savings accounts than big banks.	ATMs can be harder to find. Tend to be local, so not the best choice if you plan to move. Customer service can be sketchy.
Online/Discount Brokerage	Complete set of investment choices and low trade fees. Provide online and phone support.	Don't offer personalized financial advice. May or may not have branch offices.

Financial Institution	Pros	Cons
Full-service Brokerage	Offer wide range of financial planning and advice.	Higher trade fees. Beware of sales commission.
Mutual Fund Company specialize in the funds that they manage	Full range of account types and brokerage services. Best rates when you purchase from their fund family.	Typically have $1000+ limit for buying a mutual fund
Small Banks	Physical offices. You can establish a relationship with your banker.	May offer fewer services.
Big Banks, the well known ones you see around town	Lots of ATMs. Lots of branch offices.	Fees, hidden fees, surprise penalties, terrible interest rates, numerous scandals exposing how they rip off consumers.

I ♥ online banks for college students. When you are living off a debit card, they provide all the liquidity you need without fees. Some, but not all, offer a full range of savings and Roth IRA choices.

I ♥ credit unions for their honest mission statement, low fees and auto loans, but investment choices are limited and you will soon outgrow what they have to offer.

I ♥ discount brokers because they offer a wide range of investment choices and account types that you can grow into. Maybe all you need right now is a Roth IRA but later you may want an account for trading stocks, a 429 savings plan for your children, and a Solo 401(k) for your own business. You can conveniently do all this at one brokerage.

Financial institution comparison

There are many banks and financial institutions and only you can pick what is right for you. But I want you to be aware of the possibilities and have good choices.

Keep in mind that the U.S. inflation rate today, as I am making this table, is 1.8%. That means any account with an interest rate lower than 1.8% is falling behind on your spending power. Why would you agree to such a low interest rate on your bank account? Mainly for three reasons: (1) the convenience of moving money between checking and savings, (2) because the money is going to be used very soon and the interest rate is inconsequential, or (3) you haven't got around to finding a better investment.

I've looked up the services and interest rates from a few well-known financial institutions and I've noted the interest rates of the default savings account, just as a point of comparison, so you can get a feel for how much these accounts vary.

Key for the following table:

★★   Excellent choice - best of class

★   Good choice - meets our criteria for no fees and good investment options

✓   This service is offered and rates will vary

∅   Poor choice - limited services, extra fees, low returns, or high minimums

Institution	Checking/debit	Regular savings	Long term goal	Roth IRA	Investment account	Auto loans
Ally (online bank and brokerage)	★	★★ 1.90%	★	★	★	✔
CapitalOne (online bank)	★	★ 1.00%	Ø	Ø		✔
Charles Schwab (discount brokerage)	★★	★ 0.50%	★	★	★	
Credit Unions (national average)	★	★ 0.17%		Ø		✔
TDAmeritrade (discount brokerage)		★	★	★	★	
Vanguard or Fidelity (mutual fund co. and brokerage)		★	★	★	★	
Sallie Mae (money market acct)		★★ 2.15%	★			
Big banks	Ø	Ø	Ø	Ø	Ø	Ø

Do your own investigation.

☐ Look up the "current US inflation rate." (Without this you don't really know if you are getting a decent interest rate.)

☐ Compare the current interest rates on savings accounts at yours and other banking institutions at https://www.bankrate.com/banking/savings/rates/ Adjust the "minimum deposit amount" to get rid of the high rollers. Read the reviews on the banks that interest you.

☐ Audit your current accounts

    ☐ Are you being charged a maintenance fee?

    ☐ Are you signed up for overdraft protection? You probably want to cancel it. Overdraft protection is a big profit maker for banks. You overcharge your debit card by $1 and they stick you with a $25 fee! Better to have the card declined than to rack up those fees.

☐ How does your savings interest rate compare to the other offerings?

Now you have a good view of how your current accounts match up against other financial institutions. You will have to decide which factors are most important to you and pick the bank and brokerage that best meet your needs.

Banking summary

You are ready to choose your financial institutions. Let's turn all this analysis and research into some action. What you choose now will probably meet your needs for years, but there is nothing stopping you from changing financial institutions at some future date. People do it all the time. So let's move forward with no fear.

☐ Choose a financial institution for your checking and savings. You can stick with your current bank or take the time to switch to something better. Don't spend too much time chasing interest rates. The difference between a low rate of 0.10% and a high rate of 1.90% is only $18 per year on every $1000 on deposit. On the other hand, a monthly maintenance fee will really add up over time, so avoid it.

☐ Choose a brokerage or mutual fund company that will be home to your future goal account, Roth IRA, and investment account. You might not need them all now, but you will soon.

    ☐ Open the accounts you are ready to start funding. Check the minimum deposit requirements.

    ☐ Don't be intimidated by the account application form. Use the online/phone support to help you through the process. They want your business so they will be very helpful!

    ☐ The brokerage will ask if you want a "margin account." Say No. This would allow you to buy stock on credit and we will not be doing that.

☐ Link your brokerage accounts to your checking account so it will be easy to move money.

4

AUTOMATION

Hooray! You have a spending budget, some savings goals, and accounts at financial institutions that are going to give you the services and choices you deserve. Let's put that all together so you don't have to waste time on ordinary tasks. The key to our success and future wealth is to automate everything that is boring. We will get your money flowing to all the right places and then we will be ready to pick some investments.

Spending, saving & banking all working together

Checking

- ☐ Set up auto-deposit for your paycheck to your checking account. (Your workplace has a form for you to fill out and they will need the routing and account numbers off a check.)
- ☐ Set up low-balance alerts for your checking account.
- ☐ Turn off overdraft protection (unless it is free)

☐ Set up automatic payments for all your bills to come out of your checking account right after you get paid.

Emergency Fund

☐ Schedule automatic transfers of money from your checking account to the savings account you will use for your emergency fund.

Roth IRA

☐ Decide if your Roth IRA will be administered by your workplace or your brokerage.

    ☐ If the Roth IRA is through your work, set up your automatic contributions

    ☐ If the Roth IRA account is at a brokerage, set up automatic transfers from your checking account to the Roth IRA account.

Future Goal Fund

☐ Schedule automatic transfers of money from your checking account to the savings account you will use for your future goal fund. This is likely a brokerage account because we are going to want the investment choices available there.

☐ If you have more than one future goal with different time horizons, you can handle this a number of ways:

    ☐ Open multiple accounts (not a problem at a no-fee, no-minimum institution)

    ☐ Use a feature that lets you divide the account into different named buckets (a feature at some institutions)

    ☐ Keep the funds together in one account and keep track of the division.

☐ Give your goal funds inspiring names.

Investment account

☐ If you have allocated money toward your brokerage investment account, schedule those automatic transfers from your checking account.

Flexible spending

☐ What is left in your checking account will be the money that you are free to spend for things that bring you joy, confident that you have paid your bills and are saving for the future.

☐ If you have a hard time controlling your flexible spending, use your debit card, not your credit card, so you never go over your planned budget.

☐ Some people find that limiting their flexible spending to only cash transactions makes them more conscious of how they are spending and less likely to overspend. Try that if it helps you.

Great job, your money is flowing to all the right places to support your financial goals.

Don't stop now. Some people get bogged down when it comes to making investment decisions, but it is easier than you think. Our next step is to pick great investments that will grow the money you have so thoughtfully assigned to your different accounts.

5

INVESTING

Stepping into the world of investing can seem daunting. This is the point where most people hyperventilate and run away. You might think it is only for rich people who share investment secrets and you could never know enough to compete with them. That's all an illusion.

Investing isn't the same as picking stocks. Financial news shows spend a lot of time talking about individual company stocks, not because it's the best place to invest, but because it is dramatic. Lots of drama and unpredictability is entertaining for their show, but we are here to make money. We will not be influenced by talking heads (mostly old white guys) with dubious motivations. They are not helpful and we don't need them.

Fear not, this will be easy. We are going to seek out investment strategies that are uncomplicated, balance risk and reward, and grow steadily over long periods of time. We will set our plans in motion and let our bank accounts grow with minimal fuss.

Why invest?

Inflation has been unusually stable during your adult lifetime, averaging about 2% per year, which means the average cost of goods increases by 2% annually and it takes more dollars to buy the exact same things you bought last year. It also means doing nothing with your money is like withdrawing 2% every year and lighting it on fire. Clearly, we need a better plan than that.

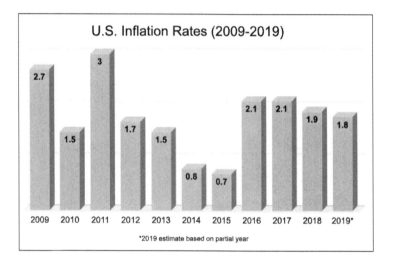

Our plan is to invest in a way that balances earnings and risk and takes advantage of the fact that you are very young and have a lot of years to let your long-term investments grow. You are so lucky to be starting to invest now in your life. It's like you are competing in the marathon at the Olympics except you get a one-week head start. It doesn't matter how fast the other competitors are, you will come out ahead.

Our philosophy is Buy And Hold. We will choose high quality, long-term investments and let the money grow. We aren't chasing the stock market and we aren't reacting to the news. Lots of people have lost lots of money thinking they could outwit the markets and predict what will happen next. We have faith that the markets rise over time and we are taking advantage of that fact.

Risk tolerance

The truth about investing is that sometimes you will earn money and sometimes you will lose money. Riskier investments come with greater upside and downside. We are going to manage that by balancing your portfolio so that some things go up when other things go down, smoothing out your overall return so you don't feel like you are on a rollercoaster.

How would you feel if the stock market dropped 20% in one week and your account value dropped that much? Could you stick to your strategy and be patient? No matter how you invest, you need to be able to stomach some ups and downs. Unless you pick investments that earn barely anything, you *will* suffer short-term losses. You need to be psychologically prepared for this, with confidence in your investment decisions, so you can stay the course.

The classic investment mistake when a down market spooks you:

1. Ignore your long term strategy and sell your investments
2. Watch the market flail, uncertain when to reinvest
3. Realize the market recovered and you missed your chance to invest when it was low
4. Now you are holding uninvested cash and the market prices are higher than when you sold. Your position is worse than if you had done nothing.

On the other hand, maybe you have a very high tolerance for risk and want to invest in wildly risky schemes. That could be very rewarding, or very costly, but certainly will give you an education. In "Level 4" investing I talk about allocating some play money to explore the wilder side of investing.

Take an Investment Risk Tolerance Quiz

This is optional. Reflect on your risk personality. These two quizzes ask the same questions: the first is self-scored and the second is automated but asks for more personal information. Choose one to complete and reflect on how much risk fits with your personality.

https://njaes.rutgers.edu/money/assessment-tools/investment-risk-tolerance-quiz.pdf

http://pfp.missouri.edu/research_IRTA.html

Level 1 Investing - Safe and just keeping up with inflation

Your emergency fund should be in an account that earns some interest and is easy to access on short notice if you should need the cash. If your Future Goal fund is something you will be accessing within a couple years, it is also a candidate for a super safe investment strategy.

Low-risk, easy access investment choices for your emergency or future goal funds include:

- The savings account linked to your checking account, which is probably earning less than the inflation rate, is very safe because it is insured by the federal government.

- A money market deposit account is a special type of savings account offered by banks and credit unions. The benefits are a higher interest rate (not always) and check writing capability, but you have to meet a minimum deposit and are limited on the number of transactions per month.

- Money market funds (MMF) invest in short term, high credit quality securities to produce moderate but reliable returns. You have access to these through brokerages and mutual fund companies.

- Interest earning checking accounts earn such a small amount that they are not a good place to keep your savings.
- A CD (certificate of deposit) is something old people like. It locks in an interest rate for a fixed number of months and you can't access the money during that time. You don't need a CD if you pick a MMF with a similar rate of return plus you will still have access to the money in a MMF.

If your savings is small, less than $1000, then your default savings account is fine. Chasing an additional 1% of interest will earn you at most $10 a year. Don't stress over that.

If your savings is large and growing, the extra earnings will be beneficial, so you might as well set up a good savings investment choice. The best combination of low risk and decent rates for short-term savings is in money market funds.

Choose a money market fund

A good money market fund (MMF) will earn more than the current inflation rate. MMFs must be actively bought or sold through your brokerage, like other securities. It can take up to one day to complete a buy or sell, so you will have to plan ahead when you want to take cash out.

You are looking for something that fits your risk tolerance and time horizon. You will need to research the MMFs offered by your particular brokerage. This is your first step into buying and selling funds. You are becoming an investor!

When you research money market funds at your brokerage (use their search tool), you will probably see a short list.

☐ Look for a "retail" or "prime" taxable money fund. (Tax-exempt funds earn a lower return and make the most sense for people in high tax brackets. Government money funds are marginally safer than prime money funds and earn marginally less, which you can choose if you are super risk averse.)

- ☐ Check that you meet the minimum deposit requirement.
- ☐ Click on the Buy button. This will take you to the trading screen.
    - ☐ Enter the amount you want to invest.
    - ☐ You probably want to choose "reinvest dividends and capital gains." That means the account keeps growing in the same investment instead of generating uninvested cash in the account.
- ☐ Click on Review Order. Verify that there is no transaction fee. Read the notes to see if there are restrictions on how soon you can sell.
- ☐ Confirm the order

Congratulations on making your first investment. If you need to withdraw some of the money, you will go back to the trading screen and choose Sell.

Level 2 Investing - Lifecycle funds

MMFs are great for your short-term savings, but if you are saving for a goal that is decades away, like your retirement, you can make more money through other types of investments. You have the advantage of time, which lets you ride the ups and downs of the stock market and come out way ahead in the end.

I want you to invest in the stock market, and not in just one stock (that would be risky) but in thousands of stocks so that bad news in one industry doesn't destroy your portfolio. Choosing and buying 1,000+ stocks would be a lot of work, so we will rely on **mutual funds** which pool money from many investors allowing the fund to invest in hundreds or thousands of stocks and bonds that fit a particular theme. Now we are right back to the same problem that there are thousands of mutual funds and how do we pick the good ones? Let's rely on statistics. The data shows us that low-fee funds perform just as well or better than high-fee funds, so we want low fees. **Index funds** are a particular type of mutual fund that hold stock in proportion to one of the well known financial indexes (e.g., the S&P 500 index is a measure of 500 large company stocks). Index funds are great because they typically have low fees and an investment strategy that is easy to understand. Cheap and easy -- that's our motto.

Your perfect portfolio would be a collection of index funds: a mix of large, medium, small and international indexes plus some real estate and bonds funds. I'm already boring you, right? So let's make this really simple...

Lifecycle Funds, or Target-Date Funds, do all the work of creating a balanced portfolio. Tell them when you want to retire (or cash out) and they choose an investment mix of mutual funds that create the appropriate asset allocation for you. If your retirement date is 40 years away, they will pick a mix of aggressive high-yield investments. As time passes and your retirement date grows nearer, they adjust the asset allocation to be more conservative.

Lifecycle Fund advantages are
- It's easy to get started investing
- You only have to make one choice to get a diversified set of investments
- The mix of investments (asset allocation) automatically changes over time to be appropriate for your time horizon
- Rebalancing is done for you
- Most have low expense ratios
- Most are tax efficient, that is they don't do excessive selling that generates taxable events

Reasons not to choose a lifecycle fund
- Your goals aren't date based
- You don't like the fund's investment choices

- You don't like the asset allocation
- You want more control over taxable events
- You want to invest in things besides mutual funds

Your 401(k), Roth IRA and brokerage investment accounts are all great candidates for a lifecycle fund investment. These accounts might be at different institutions with different offerings, so you will have to repeat this research work. Go to the online investment research center and search on "Target-Date 20xx" with your retirement year filled in and see what each has to offer you. A typical 401(k) plan will offer just one choice for each target date. An investment account at Schwab might offer ten funds for the year you choose. Click into the fund description and study the specifics.

When choosing a Target-Date mutual fund look at these key factors:

☐ Net Expense Ratio should be less than 0.75%. I've seen as low as 0.08%. I've also seen outrageously high expense ratios, so do look before buying.

☐ Loads and fees are extra charges that we don't want. I noticed a Wells Fargo Target-Date fund that charges a front-end load of 5.75% which means for every $1000 you invest, they take $57.50 right off the top as a commission for the salesperson. That's outrageous. No loads!

☐ Check that it is open to new investors, which most lifecycle funds are.

☐ Is there a minimum starting investment? Save up until you meet the minimum.

Here are some examples of Target-Date fund families that meet all our requirements and are from reliable companies:

- Fidelity Freedom, $0 minimum
- Schwab Target, $0 minimum
- T. Rowe Price Retirement, $0 and $2500 minimums
- Vanguard Target Retirement, $1000 minimum

Since the typical Target-Date fund has no loads (no buy and sell fees) there is no danger in jumping in. They often do have short-term redemption fees, typically 90 days, so plan on leaving your money in place for 3 months at least. If you find a fund you like even better, you can eventually move your money at no cost, so don't be afraid to start. But overall, your goal is to leave this money invested for a long time.

Level 3 Investing - Customizing your portfolio

If you are not satisfied with lifecycle funds and want to make your own decisions, then you are ready for the next level of investing. But I have to warn you, this is a big step up from choosing a lifecycle fund. This may be worth your time and energy if you have more than $50,000 to invest or if the lifecycle allocations totally mismatch your goals.

The minimal work you will need to do:

1.   Choose an asset allocation.
2.   Research and choose 3 to 7 index funds to match your asset allocation.
3.   Buy the funds
4.   Once or twice a year, rebalance your account by buying and selling funds until you achieve your asset allocation again
5.   Every 5 years, reconsider your asset allocation in terms of your investment horizon and adjust your investments

Besides all the research and decision-making, you will also need the discipline to keep buying and rebalancing even when the market takes a dip or a particular fund is doing badly. If losing money stresses you out and causes you to panic and sell, then your investment strategy is not going to work and you will earn less than if you had put it into a lifecycle fund and ignored it. You must commit to a strategy.

Asset allocation

After all those warnings you are still reading this section? You are brave, so let's continue.

The first step is to decide on your asset allocation. A handy way to see examples of asset allocation and fund choices is to click into the "Holdings" section of a Target-Date fund. You can see exactly how they are distributing their investment choices. Each Target-Date fund will be a little different but they have the same overall goal -- balance risk and reward for the given time period.

Sample simplified asset allocation

Investing for your retirement this many years in the future	Investment allocation
40 years	70% US stocks 25% non-US stocks 5% bonds
30 year	65% US stocks 25% non-US stocks 10% bonds
20 years	50% US stocks 25% non-US stocks 25% bonds
10 years	40% US stocks 18% non-US stocks 35% bonds 7% cash

The table shows us that a person who is 40 years away from needing their retirement money will be heavily invested in the stock market. As the retirement date nears, stock funds shift to more bond funds to reduce risk. But there are many more factors that go into picking your funds. Within those categories of US and non-US stocks you have to allocate between large-, mid-, and small-cap stock funds and funds from developed-world and emerging markets. Likewise, there are a great variety of bond funds with varying risks and rewards. And I've not included real estate funds (REITs), which are part of most portfolios.

You need to find the asset allocation that is right for you. You might need more than one if you have some highly differentiated goals, such as a house down payment account that you will access within 10 years and a retirement account you won't touch for 40 years. They need to be treated differently so the money is there when you need it. I encourage you to read more blogs, articles and books on the topic of asset allocations.

To play around with a simple asset allocation tool, try this one from Vanguard. The results are not highly personalized, but it asks good questions for you to think about. https://personal.vanguard.com/us/FundsInvQuestionnaire

Research index funds

Once you choose your asset allocation, you have to choose individual mutual funds to achieve the allocation goal. My favorite type of mutual fund is an Index Fund, designed to emulate a particular market index by owning all the corresponding stocks or bonds.

Key features of an Index Fund are

- Passive management, in contrast to actively managed funds where professionals are paid to make *buy* and *sell* decisions. Securities are automatically bought or sold to best emulate the index.
- Superior returns compared to actively managed funds. You pay extra to have fund managers trying to beat the

indexes, but they fail 80% of the time, so why pay extra for that?

• Lower expense ratios than managed funds, and that means more money stays in your account.

• Breadth of holdings, as dictated by the index being followed, means the fund owns hundreds or thousands of securities, which is usually more than a managed fund would buy, thus reducing risk.

• Fewer taxable transactions than most actively managed funds which means you have more control over when to sell and pay the taxes on your profit.

Don't interpret this as meaning index funds are a sure thing. In the long term, they tend to produce reliable results. But in the short term an index fund can lose money like any other investment. For example, the "S&P 500" is a popular index that tracks 500 large U.S. company stocks. It is popular because it has earned an average of 8% return over a long period of time. But it has had some really rough years, even within your lifetime. From 2000 to 2002 the S&P 500 lost 46% of its value, in 2008 it lost 38%, and in 2018 was down 6%. Those were hard times for investors. Sticking to an investment strategy was emotionally difficult during that phase. If you are buying individual funds you are going to see both ups and downs and you need the strength to handle it.

Beyond Index funds

If choosing from only index funds feels too limiting, you can start researching the multitude of other available mutual funds. Your 401(k) will have a limited selection and you will need to work within those parameters for that account. Your other savings and investment accounts will have a much broader selection.

There may be thousands of mutual funds offered by your brokerage, index funds being just a small subset of that. You can use the brokerage's search tool to find funds that align with your particular goals.

Key criteria for your mutual fund search should include

☐ Net expense ratio, the lower the better since it is deducted from your account and eats away at your profit. Be skeptical of funds that have an expense ratio higher than these 2018 averages:

- 0.15% S&P 500 index funds
- 0.20% other index funds
- 0.75% bond funds
- 1.00% large-cap stock funds
- 1.10% mid-cap stock funds
- 1.20% small-cap stock funds
- 1.25% foreign stock funds

☐ No-loads. A front-end or back-end load is an extra fee you pay when you buy or sell a fund, generally used as a commission to someone. There is no evidence that Load funds perform better the No Load funds, so don't waste your money.

☐ No 12b-1 fees, which are used to cover the fund's marketing costs.

☐ If a broker, advisor or bank employee is trying to convince you to buy a fund with high fees, assume they are on commission. There is no reason to believe their fund will perform better than a low cost fund. Past fund performance is not a guarantee of future performance. Fund managers sometimes close poor performing funds to make their fund averages look stronger. Be suspicious of everything with high fees.

Both index funds and actively managed funds reduce risk by building a diverse investment portfolio, but neither one is a sure thing. If the fund is heavily invested in stocks and the whole stock market goes down, your account value will go down. The key to long term investing and reaping high returns is the ability to ride through the rough times.

Variations on mutual funds include:

- Exchange Traded Funds (ETFs) are like an index fund in that they hold all the stock represented by the index, but you buy and sell them through a brokerage like they are stock. ETFs may have lower management fees and lower initial investment requirement than the equivalent mutual fund. These can be an excellent choice, so compare them to their mutual fund counterpart.

- Socially Responsible Mutual Funds buy stock from companies that meet environmental or social criteria declared by the fund. These tend to be "actively managed" funds requiring professional investors to make choices, and therefore have higher fees than passively managed funds.

- Fixed Income Funds invest in high yield bonds to generate a steady stream of income, favored by retired people, but not by people avoiding taxes.

- Balanced Funds invest in a mix of stock and bonds giving you an instant asset allocation if you can find a mix that fits your needs. Target-Date funds are an example of this.

- Real Estate Investment Trusts (REIT) own many kinds of income-producing commercial real estate.

- Bond funds invest in fixed income or debt securities of corporations or governments and are generally considered more stable than stock funds. The quality rating and the yield will be clues to how safe or risky a particular fund is. Some bond funds are exempt from federal or local taxes, which can be useful to people in high tax brackets.

Buy, rebalance, rebalance, rebalance

Now that you've decided on an asset allocation and researched mutual funds, you are ready to buy your investment in the proportions that match your allocation target. To create a diversified portfolio you will need at least seven funds. To duplicate a lifecycle fund you will need to choose 10 to 20 mutual funds.

After buying, set calendar reminders to rebalance your portfolio, probably twice a year, so that you buy and sell funds to invest the extra cash you have accumulated and get back to your target allocations. Without rebalancing, your account will drift into a different allocation that might not match your goals.

Creating your own asset allocation and choosing your investments is obviously a lot of work, but totally worth it if you have millions of dollars. You and I both know you will get there some day, but please don't worry about rushing into this phase of investing if you are a beginner. There is plenty of time to build your knowledge and transition from simple lifecycle funds to your own investment mix.

Level 4 Investing - The Thrill of the Stock Market

You may have the view that "real" investing means buying and selling individual company stocks. It's the exciting stuff of company founders getting rich and movies about Wall Street. You may believe it's a great get-rich-quick scheme, you just need to find the right stock that goes up 100 times in value and you will be wealthy! It's much like the gambling lure. The news stories are about the one person who struck it rich, but ignore the many who lost money.

> INVESTING IN INDIVIDUAL STOCKS IS
> TOO MUCH WORK!

For more than 20 years I've been in an investment club that buys and sells stocks with the goal of making a profit. The benefit of being in a club is that you have ten times the ideas for stocks to investigate and ten times the person-power to do the investigations. Buying stock that will appreciate is a hard job that requires tons of research and then ongoing monitoring so that you sell at the right time. Our club has been happy with our results, beating the S&P 500 index most of those years. Here is my number one learning from decades of buying and selling stocks: Doing it well takes lots of time and effort.

If you are the type of person that loves reading the financial news and doing the research into companies, then buying and selling stock could be a way for you to make money. But it will take waaaaaaaay more time than buying mutual funds, you will be less diversified, and you will be more likely to lose money.

You still have the bug? Still want the excitement of owning individual stocks? Or maybe something completely different, like cryptocurrency? People like you can establish a play fund that is a small percentage of your total portfolio. It's a lot like people that go to Vegas and decide how much money they are allowed to gamble with. You go in with the acceptance that you could lose it all. Given your level of experience, you probably will lose some of it. Good for you if you come out ahead. There will be ups and downs and you will learn a lot. Choose a brokerage, try your hand at trading individual stocks, and set up a system to evaluate your returns.

ESPP

If you are participating in an Employee Stock Purchase Plan (ESPP) then you are already in the stock market. You are buying stock at some consistent interval and you will be faced with the question of when to sell the stock. Most people fall into one of these groups:

1. The Hold Forever strategy: A popular course of action is to hold the ESPP stock hoping the price will go up forever. This strategy has three benefits: you don't have to make any decisions, you don't have to deal with taxes on the profit, and you get to dream about getting rich. If this was a sure thing, I wouldn't have any other advice to

offer you, but it is not a sure thing. Stock goes up and down in every company eventually, so doing nothing means taking on a lot of risk and missing the opportunity to diversify.

2. The Sell Everything strategy: I have a friend who used to sell all his ESPP shares on the day he received them, locking in immediate profit (because the strike price is always less than the current market price), and reinvested all that money in a diversified portfolio. In the end, the company and the stock did tank and he looked like a genius, but while the stock was on the rise, everyone else thought he was crazy. In the end, he made quite a lot of money.

3. ABS (Always Be Selling) strategy: A compromise position is to regularly sell some of your holdings to reinvest in a diversified way. Sometimes you will catch the high price and sometimes you won't, so you have to let go of the idea that you can predict the movement of the stock market. In the end, you will have a large, diversified portfolio.

Tax treatment may or may not influence the timing of your sales. Stock held more than two years after the beginning of the offering window will be taxed at a long-term capital gains rate instead of the ordinary income rate. If you are in a low tax bracket, this difference is small. High earners have more to gain by considering long-term capital gains trade-offs. Use tax software to run both scenarios to compare the difference and see if it is relevant to your situation.

If your ESPP stock makes up your entire investment portfolio then I urge you to consider diversifying by selling some shares and buying some index funds. Having one company control both your paycheck and your life savings is the opposite of being diversified. Regardless of how great you think your company is today, diversification protects you from all kinds of surprising changes.

When to hire a professional

If you have accumulated a significant amount of money and are not comfortable or interested in making your own financial decisions, you may want to enlist the help of a professional advisor.

☐ Regardless of what title they have, only hire and take advice from a "fiduciary". They are legally required to give you advice in your best interest. They are paid on an hourly or "percent of funds under management" basis, not on commission. If your advisor works on commission then they are heavily incentivized to direct you to investments that are best for them, not you.

☐ Ask your friends, family and coworkers if they can recommend a financial advisor.

☐ Research your candidates on these web sites: napfa.org, finra.org, sec.org

☐ Have a meeting to interview the advisor for what services they offer, whether your styles are compatible, what training they have, and what they charge. Ask them "Do you work to the fiduciary standard at all times?" If they evade the question, run away.

☐ Take it one step further and ask them to sign the "Fiduciary Oath" which you can print from www.thefiduciarystandard.org

☐ Robo-advisors are becoming ever more popular and could be a low cost solution for you, but all the same standards apply: Is it providing the services you need and acting as a fiduciary? Research robo-advisors online and interview friends who have used them.

☐ Choose a qualified advisor and decide how often you will meet.

Investing summary

Now that you've seen the choices and matched them to your goals and risk tolerance, it's time to make your investments. Don't be hesitant or overwhelmed. You are well equipped to make some easy decisions now that you can change later when you have more money. Persevere!

- ☐ Your **Emergency Fund** is probably in the savings account attached to your checking account earning 0% to 2% interest. Moving it to a money market fund earning more than the current inflation rate is optional. Consider again when you have accumulated more in that account.
- ☐ Your **Future Goal Fund** investment choice should be compatible with how soon you need the money:
    - ☐ A goal 1-4 years in the future should be in something non-volatile, like a money market fund earning more than inflation.
    - ☐ A 5+ year goal could be invested in a target-date fund set for 5 years from now. Stick with a MMF if you don't want to take any risk.
    - ☐ A 10 year goal fund could be in a target-date fund set for 10 years from now.
- ☐ Your **401(k)** will have limited choices, as will your **Roth IRA** if it is hosted by your workplace, so for someone so young, your best bet is one, or a mix, of these:
    - ☐ Target 2060 or 2050 Fund depending on when you hope to retire (though 2060 and 2050 funds look pretty identical at this early stage)
    - ☐ S&P 500 or Large Cap Index fund if you are feeling quite aggressive and could stay calm if your investment fell 30% in one year.

- ☐ If your **Roth IRA** is at a brokerage, you will have many investment choices, but that account will start out small so I recommend simplicity.
  - ☐ Pick a Target 2060 or 2050 Fund and let it ride.
- ☐ Your **investment account** will be small in the beginning but we expect it to grow over time.
  - ☐ Start with a lifecycle fund, like a Target 2050 or 2060. Get your money working for you immediately.
  - ☐ If you are interested in a more personalized investment strategy, start doing the research to pick your asset allocation and funds. As money accumulates in the account you can move it from the lifecycle fund to the individual funds you have chosen. Keep doing that until you achieve your asset allocation goal.
- ☐ **Automate investing of new cash.** You have already set up automatic transfers to your different kinds of savings accounts but you also want that money invested.
  - ☐ See if deposits can be automatically swept into an investment choice.
  - ☐ If an automatic investment feature is not available, set up monthly or quarterly calendar reminders to look at your account and move money into your investments.

6

CREDIT RATING

Why is it important?

There is this mysterious thing called your Credit Rating that you need to care about if you want to get the best deals. Your credit rating is being created behind the scenes and can affect the loan rates you are offered, whether you can get a credit card, and even potential employers or landlords might look it at. It's super important, yet most of us have no idea how it is calculated or how to improve it.

How to find your credit rating

There are two parts to your credit rating: a Credit Report and a Credit Score (a.k.a. FICO score). The Report is a profile on your financial history that tracks your loans, credit cards and maybe your rent, and flags every time you've been late with a payment. The Score is a number generated from all the information in your Credit Report.

	Credit Report	**Credit Score**
Cost to see it	Free once a year	$20 or free estimate
Includes	List of creditors Payment history Late payments Amount of loans Credit inquiries by others	A number that represents your credit risk. 720-850 best 700-719 very good 675-699 good 620-674 mediocre 560-619 poor Below 560 worst
Why check?	If there are errors, you can fix them. If you are a victim of fraud, you can verify you've cleaned up your record.	Your score predicts how good a loan rate you will be offered.
How to check	annualcreditreport.com	myfico.com to pay $20; creditsesame.com for a free estimate

Credit report

You can access your Credit Report for free, once a year, from each of the three agencies (Equifax, Experian, and TransUnion) that each do exactly the same job and should have the same information. It's good to rotate through the three over time to make sure one hasn't made an error. Sadly, errors are quite common, due to both simple mistakes and identity theft, and can take months to remedy. Verify your information is accurate and if you find a mistake submit a dispute right away. Don't wait until the day before you are going to ask for a loan or fill out a rental application to find out your credit report has issues.

Credit score

Your Credit Score is harder to access than your Credit Rating. These agencies all charge money to show you your actual score generated by their "proprietary formula." An estimated score from CreditSesame might be good enough to show that you are in the range you were expecting or that you are improving, but it's a free service and makes no guarantees as to consistency with the official agencies. If you have no loans and no credit cards, you might not even have a score. Read below to check and improve your score.

The average credit score for someone age 21-34 is 634, which falls into the "mediocre" range. A four-year car loan for this person could have an interest rate 5% higher than for someone in the "best" range of 720+. Someone with a score in the "worst" range will pay 5% more in interest than the person with the "mediocre" score. The difference can be large and you will save a lot of money in interest payments if you can move your score to that "best" range. It might take you 1-2 years of good financial behavior to get your score from "mediocre" to "good" and up to 7 years to achieve a "best" score. Be patient and keep paying your bills on time.

If you are applying for a home loan, it is worthwhile to pay to see your actual Credit Score from the agencies. Find out which agency the loan provider will be using or pay for all three. $20 per score is a small price to pay to avoid a surprise and save thousands of dollars in interest payments.

Be aware that the agencies push their Identity Protection monthly subscription on their web sites and it's hard to find the option to pay for your score one time. Try looking in "Products" and "One-time Credit Report". We are all becoming paranoid about identity theft these days, but resist the identity protection subscription. You can achieve the same thing by checking your report annually for free.

Steps to improve your credit rating

Your Credit Score (FICO score) calculation is based on a number of factors that reflect your credit worthiness. If you want your score to improve, do these things:

- ☐ Order your free credit reports from the 3 agencies and look for errors or fraud. If you find mistakes, file a dispute.
- ☐ Pay rent, loans and credit cards on time (35% of your FICO score is reliability)
- ☐ Hold and use at least one credit card for a long time (15% of your FICO score reflects length of credit history)
- ☐ Improve your "credit utilization rate" by paying down your credit cards and asking your card company to raise your limit (30% of your FICO score for credit utilization rate)
- ☐ Have a variety of credit types, such as credit cards and loans (10% for variety)
- ☐ Pace yourself on applications for new credit cards or loans (10% for not going crazy with applying for new ways to get into debt)

The bottom line is DO get a credit card, use it responsibly, pay it off every month, and hold it for a long time. Don't run out and get a loan or a bunch of credit cards just to boost your score. A great credit score is built slowly over a long period of time.

Caution:
- • Don't get a credit card or raise your limit if you don't feel you can control your spending. Great scores only come from paying off your cards consistently.

- Don't apply for a bunch of cards all at once in an attempt to improve your credit utilization rate. Applying for multiple cards hurts your credit score for a few months.
- Don't panic if you make a mistake and miss a payment. Your score will take a temporary hit but it will recover in a few months if you get back on track and pay it off every month.
- Keep your oldest credit card if it does not have an annual fee. Your oldest card will probably determine the length of your credit history and older is better.
- Pay off your full balance before closing a credit card. Better yet, pay it off but don't close the account, just cut up the card. That will help with your credit utilization rate.

The truth about credit cards

Do you want a credit card? Do you need a credit card?

The positive sides of credit cards are:

- They help you build your credit rating
- They are handy if you get in a temporary financial jam.
- They offer cash back and travel rewards that could be valuable to you

The downsides to credit cards are:

- They can make it too easy to spend more than you can afford
- They can become insanely expensive if you don't pay the full bill monthly
- Being in credit card debt can take a big emotional toll

I want you to have a credit card for all the good reasons but you need to honestly evaluate yourself and how you handle credit. Can you pass this test?

☐ Yes, I'm a person that will use a credit card responsibly.

☐ Yes, I will set up automatic payments so I pay off my credit card on time every month.

☐ I promise that if I fall behind on paying my credit card bill, I will stop using the card and not touch it again until I have paid it off.

Thank you for making the promise to be a good credit card holder. Now you deserve a really great credit card, which can be a little bit challenging if you are applying for the first time and have a short work history, but it's not impossible.

Credit card choices

Ideally, you have enough credit history to qualify for the best credit card for your lifestyle. Your criteria for choosing a credit card are:

☐ No annual fee.

☐ Cash back or travel points that you can use. I prefer cash back because I'm a great travel bargain shopper and I don't want to be tied to a particular airline or hotel chain. The best cash back card I have seen offers 2% back on all purchases with no annual fee. Search online for current deals.

☐ Low interest rate if you think you might carry a balance. (But please don't carry a balance. Pay it off every month or don't use it.)

If you lack credit history and don't qualify for one of these good cards, you can try a different approach.

☐ Ask the place where you bank if you qualify for a credit card. If you have automatic deposit on your paycheck, they are more likely to offer you a card.

☐ If you don't qualify for a standard credit card you can try a Secured Credit Card. That means you have to back your credit line with a cash deposit. Once you have built your credit history and secured a better card, you can cancel this card and get your deposit back.

☐ Your last resort is to be added to someone else's credit card as an "authorized user." You should be able to use this card and establish a credit history, but do ask the credit card company if they report authorized users to the credit reporting agencies. Some don't.

Credit card habits
Once you have that credit card in hand, be a good card user and build your credit rating.
☐ Pay on time every month.
☐ Pay the full amount.
☐ Review your statement monthly. If you find fraud and report it immediately, you usually get a full refund. I don't want to scare you, but credit cards are being compromised in huge numbers and you need to be vigilant. Most credit card fraud is done with many small online purchases in hope that you won't notice.
☐ Use the notification features to remind yourself about payment due dates or to alert you to unusual activity.
☐ Remember to use the reward points you are earning!

Auto loan options

A car loan may be your first adventure in shopping for a competitive loan and the first time your credit rating makes a big difference in your life. Be a savvy shopper and find the car and the loan that is best for you. Don't make the common mistake of accepting the loan terms from the dealership just because it is the easier path. They make it easy because they are making a hefty profit. If they offer you 0% financing for a fixed time, use the online loan calculator to see if you could pay the loan off within that time.

Educate yourself on auto loan choices.

☐ Get your credit score, either by the free estimate at creditsesame.com or pay for a copy of your actual score through myfico.com.

☐ Research current loan rates at www.bankrate.com/loans/auto-loans/rates/

☐ Ask your current banking institution what rate they will offer you. As a customer with a good track record and money in their bank, they might offer the best rate.

☐ Look at loans with a 36-month or 48-month term. If you can't afford the monthly payments then I'm pretty sure you are shopping for too expensive a car. Making payments for 5 or 6 years is too long a commitment and will keep you from investing that money in better ways.

☐ Don't lease. Leasing a car keeps you in an endless loop of making car payments forever.

☐ Consider buying a used car. The average new car loses 20% of its value after one year, 40% after three years. Choose a reliable brand that is two or three years old and enjoy an almost new car at a greatly reduced price.

☐ Whether you buy new or used, drive your car for a long time.

Before you go out shopping for a car, arm yourself with data and negotiation strategies by doing online research. Services like www.fightingchance.com will sell you detailed information on the actual cost of a new car, giving you power during negotiations.

Credit Summary

Now you know that your credit rating is a critical part of your financial power. Your credit score affects how much you pay in interest for your car and your home. It determines whether you qualify for the best credit cards and housing rentals. You really don't want to screw it up.

- ☐ Review your credit report once a year and dispute mistakes immediately.
- ☐ Build a strong credit score.
    - ☐ Pay all your bills and loan payments on time every month
    - ☐ Pay your credit card bill automatically and in full every month
    - ☐ Never cancel your oldest credit card
    - ☐ Ask to have your credit card limits increased
- ☐ Choose a good credit card with no annual fee and benefits you can use. And then pay it off every month.
- ☐ Set up notifications on your credit cards so you will recognize fraud when it happens.
- ☐ Before buying a car, or any major purchase that requires a loan, arm yourself with the best information:
    - ☐ Your current credit score
    - ☐ What loan rates you qualify for given your credit score
    - ☐ Complete research on the true price of the item you are buying
    - ☐ A negotiation strategy

7

TAXES

Unless you are a tax accountant, you probably don't find tax law very interesting. I agree, and I'm not going to try to turn you into a tax expert. I just want you to understand the basics of how your taxes are assessed and the levers you have to control how much you pay.

Taxes taken from your paycheck

Most people are mystified by how much is taken out of their paycheck for taxes. On your first day of work you were probably asked to complete a Form W-4 where you declared the "total number of allowances you are claiming" and that magically got turned into some amount of money being withheld for taxes.

- **Federal income tax withholding** takes the biggest chunk of money from your paycheck. The amount held out to pay your taxes will depend on how many allowances you have claimed.

- o If you are single with one job, no children, and no other income streams, then you probably chose 1 allowance.
- o If your life is more complicated than that, use the IRS' Withholding Calculator to make a more accurate estimate: www.irs.gov/W4App
- **State and local income tax withholding** are based on that same allowances number and tax rates vary depending on where you live.
- **FICA withholdings** are also called "payroll taxes" because they only apply to your wages, not income from investments. There are two parts:
  - o **Social Security** provides retirement and disability payments to people who qualify. Your contributions through your lifetime of work will go into a formula that determines your benefits when you retire. You are assessed 6.2% and your employer also pays 6.2% for a total of 12.4% of wages.
  - o **Medicare** provides hospital insurance benefits for the elderly, for which you will qualify some day. You contribute 1.45% of your wages and your workplace does the same for a total of 2.9%.
  - o If you are **self-employed** you are responsible for the entire amount of 12.4%+2.9%, but it might not apply to *all* your earnings. It's complicated. Talk to a tax professional.

Unfortunately, that's not the end of the story. Withholding from your paycheck is just an estimate of what you will owe in federal, state and local taxes. You may be under- or over-paying your taxes if your allowances are wrong, you had multiple jobs, or you had a lot of income from investments. You may want to run a tax estimate before the end of year to make adjustments and avoid a big debt or big refund.

Tax calculation example

Everyone loves to complain about paying taxes. Everyone but me. I've been to countries that don't have a robust tax system and I have to tell you that bad roads and raw sewage lose their charm really quickly. I'm totally fine with paying my taxes. But I'm not going to overpay my taxes. I plan ahead and use a tax accountant to take advantage of all the deductions that are available to me.

The federal and state tax rates are progressive, which means they change as you reach different levels of income. Let's look at a simplified example of someone's federal taxes in 2019:

Income from all sources	$70,000
401(k) contribution	-$10,000
IRS standard deductions	-$12,200
Taxable income equals	$47,800

So the first $22,200 isn't being taxed at all.

The next $9,700 is taxed at 10% =	$970
The next $29,775 is taxed at 12% =	$3573
The remaining $8,325 is taxed at 22% =	$1832
Total federal tax is	$6375

If they had not put $10,000 into their 401(k), that amount would fall into the 22% tax rate category and they would have paid an additional $2,200 in taxes. Using deductible retirement contributions to stay out of the higher tax brackets can save you thousands of dollars.

The following table shows how the tax rates for unmarried single filers change as income increases.

2019 Federal Tax Brackets for Unmarried Single Filers

Taxable Income Over	But Under	Tax Rate
$0	$9,700	10%
$9,700	$39,475	12%
$39,475	$84,200	22%
$84,200	$160,725	24%
$160,725	$204,100	32%
$204,100	$510,300	35%
$510,300		37%

Tax filing basics

Your federal and state tax forms are always due on April 15 of the following calendar year. The paperwork you need, the W-2 from your employer and various 1099s and 1098s from your banks and others, should be mailed to you by February 15. Always check your accounts online to see that you received all the forms you need for filing. (I once overlooked an online-only "supplemental" brokerage form that could save me $1000s in taxes, so I had to file an amendment for that year. What a hassle.)

Online tools make it easy to file your taxes if your situation is uncomplicated. If your AGI (adjusted gross income) is less than $34,000 you qualify for free filing software, but it is hidden from search engines, so you will need this URL: turbotax.intuit.com/taxfreedom. Everyone else has to pay from

$14.95-$79.99 for basic federal tax software and $19.95-$34.99 for basic state tax software. Read online reviews to see which product is right for you or check out your local tax preparation service if you would rather work with a human (H&R Block starts at about $59 per filing). If your taxes are complicated, talk to a professional tax accountant. They can keep you from making mistakes and often save you money.

Your tax is computed after deductions are subtracted from your income. Like 90% of all Americans, you will probably take the standard deduction of $12,200 (that's the single filer 2019 amount) and not have to do the extra work of completing Schedule A Itemized Deductions. If you exclusively work from home, you may be able to claim more deductions, but you will need to study the rules or use a professional to see what applies to your situation.

You may have heard of people "filing an extension" which sounds like an ideal situation for a procrastinator, but it really doesn't delay the work or postpone the cost. You still have to do a portion of the tax paperwork and pay your estimated tax *in full* by April 15. So really you are doing your tax filing twice in one year instead of once.

Scam warning: The IRS will never call your phone; they always send letters if they need to contact you. They really love paper. Any call or email you get claiming to be the IRS will be spam.

Tax vocabulary
- Adjusted Gross Income (AGI) - All the money you made from wages, interest, dividends, and other investments. This will not include income that went into your qualified retirement account, like a 401(k).
- Alternative Minimum Tax (AMT) - A parallel tax system for high earners (kicks in at $71,700 for singles in 2019). It was designed to prevent very high earners from claiming lots of deductions and paying little or no tax.
- Earned Income Tax Credit is a refund for workers with no children who make less than $15,270 (in 2018) and for

low-income families ($46,010 married with one child and limits go up with more children). The refund can be substantial so check if you qualify.

- Taxable Income - Your income after subtracting standard or itemized deductions from your AGI. This number gets plugged into the tax table.

Tax summary

☐ Use the IRS' Withholding Calculator if you think you need to adjust your withholding allowances (www.irs.gov/W4App)

☐ Use the tax calculator at www.dinkytown.net to make adjustments to your income and 401(k) contributions and see how it affects your final taxes. This might motivate you to put more in your retirement plan.

☐ Use tax filing software or a tax accounting professional to make sure you are getting all the deductions for which you qualify.

☐ If you are making student loan payments, you can deduct up to $2500 of interest paid per year, but it starts to phase out when your income reaches $70,000 (as of 2018).

☐ If you are self-employed, seek advice from a professional who can help you set up a retirement plan and minimize your taxes through other types of deductions.

8

LIVING WELL

Only you can define what it means to live well. You work hard for
your money and should be able to spend it on what you want. By
being selective, you can afford the things that are most important
to you and still save for the future.

> SPEND GENEROUSLY ON WHAT YOU LOVE.
>
> BE RELENTLESSLY FRUGAL ON WHAT
> YOU FEEL NEUTRAL ABOUT.
>
> ALWAYS BE SAVING.

You need to find your equilibrium between spending and
saving. I want you to be as excited about saving as you are about
an Amazon box arriving at your door. That may be overreaching a
bit. I at least want you to look at your savings and investment
account statements and smile because they keep getting bigger.

You are now equipped to handle surprises, both good and bad.

- Surprise car repair? You can dip into your emergency fund and then start building it back up.
- Invited on a trip to Mexico? You can check your vacation goal fund and immediately know if it is within your budget. Or start saving for it now.
- Received $5,000 as a bonus or gift? You can have it all -- fun now and building your financial foundation, too. You could wipe out some high interest debt or apply a big chunk to your various savings and investment accounts. Then keep 10-20% to spend now and enjoy.

Investing is probably the newest and most challenging part of this new financial life we are designing for you. Being in control of your money so that it doesn't cause you stress is important. Your savings is both a safety net and the assurance that you can afford to take chances or make big changes. Having money in your bank account gives you lots of choices.

I am a realist. I know we are all lazy when it comes to doing boring, repetitive chores. Paying bills, moving money, and reinvesting is boring and repetitive, and that's why the emphasis is on automating all our financial tasks. If you skipped the automation steps in the previous chapters, go back and do them now. When you automate your saving and investing you are compounding your good decisions and never have to feel guilty about not looking at your accounts.

One of the great benefits of being in your generation is that you have access to information about everything and you are not naive about Internet scams. You can use this information to help you through any new situation. Want to know the wholesale price of a car? Want a script for negotiating a raise? It's all at your fingertips. Use it to your advantage.

I'm sure retirement seems impossibly far away, but feel confident that the steps you take now will secure a comfortable retirement for you some day.

I hope this book has shown you that managing your money isn't mysterious or difficult. It takes a small amount of time once you have your systems set up. Continuous learning is going to give you better results over time and allow you to handle larger amounts of money as your income grows. You are ready for great things.

9

WHEN TO REVIEW YOUR PLAN

Your financial plan is designed to require a minimum amount of fuss, but you can't ignore it forever. Some maintenance is needed every 6 to 12 months to keep things rolling along nicely.

If you have one of these life events:
- Salary increase or large bonus
- Job change
- Job relocation or change in rent or house payments
- Combining your finances with a partner
- Debt payoff completed
- Initiated a major loan
- Or, one year has passed

Then it is time to do some finance maintenance:
- ☐ Update your budget, adjusting for fixed expenses and debt payment changes
- ☐ Check your Emergency Fund and if you have saved your target amount of 3 to 6 months of living expenses, you can

stop contributing to that fund. Shift that money to a different savings goal or your investment account.

☐ Request your Credit Report from at least one of the three agencies and review for errors

☐ Check your estimated Credit Score and see how you are doing compared to last year

☐ If you now have more flexible spending dollars, apply some of it to your top priorities:

    o Reducing debt

    o Maxing your Roth IRA

    o Contributing more to your investment accounts (401(k) or brokerage)

☐ If you have an investment account, check your asset allocation and rebalance. Or if you are using a lifecycle fund, see if it still meets your needs.

APPENDIX

Useful websites

www.**annualcreditreport.com** to order your annual free credit report from any of 3 agencies

www.**bankrate.com** for current rates on loans, credit cards, and bank interest

www.**creditkarma.com** for a free credit score estimate and credit card comparisons

www.**creditsesame.com** another site that offers a free credit score estimate

www.**dinkytown.net** for specialized financial calculators

www.**fightingchance.com** for detailed information on the cost of new cars, for a fee

www.**mint.com** for tracking your spending and saving

www.**morningstar.com** is a place to research a zillion index funds and mutual funds

www.**myfico.com** for your credit score from any of the 3 agencies

www.**optoutprescreen.com** is the official Consumer Credit Reporting Industry website for opting out of credit and insurance offers (finance junk mail); providing your social security number is optional

www.**studentaid.gov** for info and options on your student loan

www.thefiduciarystandard.org has more about financial advisors and a printable "Fiduciary Oath"

catalog.data.gov/dataset/national-student-loan-data-system can provide you with a complete lifecycle view of your student loans and grants from a national database

personal.vanguard.com/us/FundsInvQuestionnaire is an asset allocation tool that is fun to play with

turbotax.intuit.com/taxfreedom is the secret URL for free tax software for those who qualify

Visit **www.lisaworldpeace.com/yourmoney** for printable worksheets and checklists.

ABOUT THE AUTHOR

Why am I qualified to give you financial advice? I've been where you are. I started with zero knowledge and made lots of financial mistakes in my twenties. I want you to have the benefit of skipping past the usual mistakes for your age group. Here are some of my embarrassing mistakes when I was young:

- Bought a new car without asking my experienced friends for guidance. I read one article and thought I could outwit the car salesman. I have no idea how much I overpaid. To make things worse, I accepted the car dealership financing.
- Kept my entire life savings in my bank savings account earning almost no interest for years.
- Didn't open a Roth IRA as soon as I was eligible. Finally opened a Roth IRA, then put the whole balance in a risky stock that lost half its value.
- Paid overdraft fees at my bank (which was sort of not my fault) and then didn't even try to argue to have the fees reversed or overdraft cancelled.

I sucked at finances. And then one day it clicked. I didn't want to have this passive relationship with my money that left me unsure of what I could afford now and in the future. I started educating myself on all things financial and getting my accounts into shape. When my 20-something daughters started making their own financial decisions I realized I have decades of experience and knowledge to share with them and their peers.

I hope this common sense approach to money helps you take control of your finances and feel in control of your life. Each simple decision you make will build your knowledge and your portfolio. I'm sure you are ready to take on these challenges.

- Lisa Duncan

Made in the USA
San Bernardino, CA
25 November 2019